JUST BENEATH HOPE

THE DANCE

B. JADE

authorHOUSE®

AuthorHouse™
1663 Liberty Drive
Bloomington, IN 47403
www.authorhouse.com
Phone: 1 (800) 839-8640

Published by AuthorHouse 02/07/2019

ISBN: 978-1-5462-7942-6 (sc)
ISBN: 978-1-5462-7940-2 (hc)
ISBN: 978-1-5462-7941-9 (e)

Library of Congress Control Number: 2019901382

This book is dedicated to the American Cancer Society and all the doctors and nurses who helped Bob with his journey to recovery.

No part of this book is meant to change anyone's perception. This is Bob's story told through Brenda's writing.

Slow me down Lord!

Ease the pounding of my heart

By the quieting of my mind.

Steady my hurried pace

With a vision of the eternal reach of time.

Give me,

Amidst the confusions of my day,

The calmness of the everlasting hills.

—Wilferd A. Peterson

Bob had this prayer hanging on a clipboard in his workshop.

The page was tattered and torn.

SLOW ME DOWN, LORD

"Slow me down, Lord! Ease the pounding of my heart by the quieting of my mind. Steady my hurried pace with a vision of the eternal reach of time. Give me, amidst the confusion of my day, the calmness of the everlasting hills.

My hope is that the words that I share will help someone along the way see hope through my husband's struggle. It's the struggle of a man full of life and spirit—a Peter Pan. A man that did not want his life to be remembered by cancer treatments. In my experience with people in recovery, some of them that want to change their lives for the better try to give back something. This was my husband, Bob. He wanted to give his experience of where he was going and where he had been back to the clients in the treatment center (the program). Well, that was where I first saw Bob. He was coming from the dining hall/meeting room. He had just finished the evening lecture for family night at the center. I was working the Safe-House down below, a center for abused women, similar to the "Alive" program we have here in our county. His appearance was that of a hippie lost in the sixties. Long brown hair tied back in a ponytail. His hair did not complement his mustache even though it looked like it had not been trimmed either. He was wearing an overstarched yellow shirt, with the sleeves cuffed and rolled halfway up his arms. His blue jeans were faded but razor creased down the front. Flashback from the past and lost in the future was where my thoughts took me. He did not walk across the sidewalk or the grounds; no, Bob's walk was a bounce of energy that lifted him up. Each step was a portrait of the energy of life. I peered at him from another building. We had not met at this point. Someone had told me he was married to a woman that also worked at the center. They had both finished treatment at the center about the same time. Pattie, Bob's wife, was a staff worker there. They also informed me Pattie and Bob had gotten married shortly after they met at work. They had rules against this, but Bob did not like to follow rules. He would always find a loophole in his favor. However, the rule was two years in separation and no contact before you could date another worker. Bob was certainly a rule bender, not a sitter.

Every morning I would wake up and tell myself I won't see the reruns anymore—the View-Master clicking away with no one pushing the button or changing the slides. One reel after another. The ones I remember the most are all the episodes when Bob was sick, (There were few days when he was not sick.) They say you always reflect on the bad things before the good ones. With all my education, I cannot understand why the bad has to outweigh the good and why with so much good in our lives the View-Master keeps flicking the reel of days when I thought I could not take it anymore. View-Master, for those of you who remember, did not have sound. It was an all-silent picture. One slide after another. The pictures that run through my head are with sound. Voices, bells, sirens, life-support machines, crying, and good days of laughter. If I remember right, when I was a child I could choose where to start the slides. Right now, the episodes I am viewing are stuck. It won't go forward or backward. It just keeps flashing in my head. I believe one should have control over the memories as he or she chooses.

As I was going for a doctor appointment, I passed a woman that looked familiar to me. I stood there looking at her, and now I can't remember her name. The words came out of her mouth like hot liquid burns your mouth and the hair dryer burns if gotten too close to your ears when turned on high.

She said, "Hi." As we passed each other, she spoke. "Brenda, right?"

I know we both have put on some weight, but the faces of people I meet never leave that reel in my head. However, remembering names is not my best suit. We both shared a piece of our lives trying to catch up on what we had both missed. I told her about the injury to my ankle and why I was on a knee scooter. She shared with me about her experience on her knee scooter. Small talk.

We had gone to the same church as her and her husband, and we always sat in the same pew. When Bob and I got married, they had given us, for a wedding present, a large entrance mirror. It was a beautiful mirror. We hung it up in our living room, and when I looked at it, all the good memories would resurface—the times at church with our church family. The same church in which Bob and I were married.

I stood there looking at her, and now I can't remember her name, but her pleading, strong words flashed through my mind.

"Brenda," she said, "are you sure you want to marry this man? He is so sick, Brenda, and it would be a lot to take on in a marriage."

> Our Love
>
> We asked ourselves why we are so much alike.
>
> We have walked the same path as we listen to the same sounds.
>
> We have not just become one.
>
> We have become one beat to the same drum.

"Yes, I want to marry him."

I knew love had outweighed the need for me to look at the whole picture, but our love was strong.

Bob had gone through a liver transplant seven years before we had married. His checkups and yearly visits had all been as good as it could be. Bob was always so frail-looking, and the love for him was solid in my heart, soul, and mind. I knew we could conquer anything that came up. So there was not any doubt in my mind that this man was the man I would marry.

Bob and I both had been married before; my marriage was over after twenty-six years, and Bob's wife (Pattie) had died from cancer. It was a long struggle with the disease and death. She spent most of her time in the hospital, and it was told that Bob spent most of his time beside her. She was a beautiful and kind person. I had gotten to be friends with her and Bob at the drug center. She liked (candy) divinity, and every Christmas I would make her a Christmas tin full of it. She would always offer to pay me for it, but I wouldn't think of it. She was a staff aid, and their pay came from the bottom of the barrel.

Bob and a friend of mine would go fishing together. Bob loves to fish. He would live on the water if he could. He had told me once he had thought of getting a houseboat when he lived in Key West. He had a bass boat and a canoe. The first time we put the boat in the water, I watched him knowing with all my heart this man would not be able to do this by himself. For those of you that know nothing about putting a boat in the water, first you have to back the truck, trailer, and boat into the water. After the trailer is backed into the water, the boat is released from the trailer. The boat would be driven over to the shore to be tied up until you could pull the trailer out of the water and park the truck. I watched him, and there was never a time I did not grind my teeth. The fear was that the boat would float away before he could get into it. After several trips fishing, he started asking me to tie off the boat. The boat just seems to hang in midair, half in the water and half out. I always looked for the truck to roll into the water before the whole show was over.

One time when we were at the Osage River just outside

of Jefferson City, Missouri, Bob turned to me and said, "You

are going to drive the truck out of the water. You can do it."

My fear was that the emergency brake would fail, and I

would be in the water—truck, trailer, and me becoming one

with the river. I knew that Bob was too weak to do it all by

himself and that this could be the last fishing trip. So, after

much encouragement from the fishermen gathered next to the

truck, I jumped in, released the emergency brake, and pulled

the truck trailer and boat to the top of the hill. Everyone was

clapping by this time. Some of the fishermen even walked to

the top of the hill while clapping.

I could hear a voice from the back of the truck. Bob

was yelling, "Stop, stop, stop." I had gotten so caught up in

the moment and the fear that I wasn't listening, and I had

forgotten about Bob in the back on the boat. I just could

not believe it. Had I really done this? I knew the fear of the

truck going into the water was based on old fears of when my

neighbor backed his boat into the Mississippi with his son in

the cab. When he got out to release the boat into the water,

Brian, his son, release the air brakes. The truck, trailer, and boat sank with his son in the cab. With great effort to rescue the boy, he drowned. I am not sure if I will ever help with the boat launching again, but Bob knew at least I could pull the trailer out of the water. Bob jumped out of the boat to be a part of the cheering squad. We talked about the trip all the way home. I guess one reason I wanted to try and help him was that each day, he got weaker and weaker.

Bob always said, "When I get too weak to fish, then the quality of life is gone for me."

Our son, Tim, and Bob with his crazy hat
on. The first day of trout season.

Bob had an accident that added to his problems. A Metro bus hit him from behind, and it left him with a hematoma on his brain. His life had been altered again, but he just had so much fight in him. The first brain surgery was to release the pressure on his brain. He did not have a lot going for him because of his liver transplant, and the headaches kept getting worse. Before the surgery, he had prepared four envelopes. The envelopes would be opened one per hour. The operation was to take four hours, and he wanted me to know how much he loved me if something went wrong.

The first message read: "You can't dance without the pain."

Bob had this message on a card attached to fifteen red roses that he had delivered; fifteen was the number of years we had been friends. They came after our first date. We had gone bowling. Just two adults feeling like kids again. I did not see it as a date. Bob was always a perfect friend.

The second message read: "Don't you just feel like you're sixteen again?" This was what Bob had told me on our first date, as he called it.

The third message read: "If you are reading this, you are the most reliable person I ever meet, and I know you will be fine if something happens to me."

Bob had been a good friend for a long time. He had watched me from a distance. There were days, months, and years we stayed in contact, but Bob went through a lot after his wife died. He had even moved away for a few years. During his liver transplant, I was not a part of that stage battle for his life. I had not seen him for seven years.

The fourth message was ... before I could read it, the phone rang.

The nurse said, "The surgery went well; you can go back to see him."

Some of his family was there with me, and I wanted them to spend time with him, but they wanted me to go back first. I walked into the recovery room.

The nurse said, "He was a trooper," giving the thumbs-up.

When I reached Bob, he was laughing and carrying on about how hungry he was. I kissed him on the forehead and asked the nurse when he could eat. Bob could not last very long without eating. It was never about Jell-O and crackers. He wanted a full-course meal. I told him his family wanted to see him before they left; the nurse suggested only two at a time, but one would have to be me. His sisters Dottie and Kathy came in, and the nurse let them both visit because there wasn't anyone else in the other recovery rooms.

When they walked in Bob said, "I told you it was just another piece of cake."

They laughed, and Bob lifted his gown and flashed them. Bob was always playing jokes or kidding around. He was always playing games and causing a stir. I was embarrassed, but that was just Bob. He had a good relationship with this sister Kathy. They were close in times of need. I stayed with Bob until they moved him to a room. It was a long and tiring day. The thought of work the next day made the day seem more tiring.

Bob would go to Barnes Jewish Hospital for his checkups for his liver, but he had a different doctor for his brain surgery here at St. Clair Hospital. This was closer to our home. There was no mention of the messages Bob had given me. He didn't bring it up, so I didn't either. I did remember the last message had not been opened. As I was leaving the hospital, I took the time to sit down in the lobby to read the last letter.

I read, "I love you, and I have loved you ever since I tried the first time to share my feelings with you."

I rewound my memories back to when Bob had invited me over to cook dinner for me. Bob had called to catch up on things, and he sensed I was having a down day. That's when the dinner invite came. When I was going to leave, he had tried to talk about his feelings.

He had said, "I am just going to go out on a limb here and tell you. I am starting to have feelings for you."

He sat there on his couch wearing the white shirt and blue jeans he wore the day he climbed a ladder to check his father's roof repairs. The same jeans that showed off his cute butt and slim figure. I couldn't accept my feelings for him then, and I wasn't going to now.

I said, "You need to just climb down out of that tree. I don't want to have feelings for anyone right now."

The lobby was quiet, and I just sat there waiting for this family to reappear to say their goodbyes. Goodbye was where it always was left because they never call me to check on Bob. The relationship between his family and me was just different.

One Mother's Day when we went over to his sister Sharon's house, Bob's youngest sister, Kathy, made a comment. She said, "You are too classy of a lady for my brother."

Bob looked at me and said, "She didn't see you up to your knees in mud?"

He was referring to our fishing trip. I had to go to the bathroom so bad that Bob docked the boat against the side of the big riverbank for me to find a spot to pee. It is so much easier for men to relieve themselves. They can just go off the side of the boat. But here I was trying to climb out of the boat with my sandals still intact.

Bob offered his two cents. "You will never be able to climb up that river bluff with your shoes on. It is too slick," he said.

I knew he was right. My sandals would bog down in the shiny mud, and I would never get up that bluff. The urgency of the bathroom break grew more and more. My age had something to do with it and also being near the water. I climbed out of the boat, first my feet and then my hands to steady me. I could hear Bob laughing at my struggle. One foot and then the other foot kept getting caught in the mud. When I finally reached the top, my hands and feet were full of mud. I turned and looked for a good place to pee. All that was there was a clearing and more shiny mud to tackle. I stopped after a few steps. It just wasn't worth the walk. My hands were full of mud, and I knew I had to get my pants down. I shook my hands to try to get rid of some of the mud, but for the most part, I knew I had to do something, and my choices were slim to nothing. I squatted down for much-needed release, and just as I did, I saw something moving in the grass. It was a snake. I screamed and jumped. I don't remember which came first, the scream or me jumping.

Bob yelled, "Are you okay?"

I never answered.

He yelled again. "Are you okay?"

The pee was streaming down my legs by now. The snake did not seem to care. My feet were bogged down in the mud, and there was not a chance in hell I was going to be able to run. Quicksand was drawing me in as my pee hit the ground. I was captive to a twelve-inch yellow and black snake.

"I am okay," I screamed. "There is a snake in front of me, and I can't move!"

"What color is it?" I heard him say.

"Yellow and black," I answered.

"It won't hurt you; just don't bother it. Brenda, choose another way to come back down the hill to the boat."

Another way? I thought. I knew how deep the mud was struggling to get there (knee-deep), and now he wanted me to make new steps. I pulled my pants up and took the closest route to the boat I could without bothering the snake. *Classy*, I thought. That was the first time I was ever called classy. I looked at myself differently after that comment.

Every time Bob would tell the story, he would emphasize the word *classy*.

That was the first surgery Bob went through after his accident. He seemed to recover fast, and he even went back to work. It did not take long after that for the headaches to start again. The pressure had built up. The hematoma had to be released again. More surgery. I asked myself how much surgery his body could withstand. Bob's outlook was always good. He had survived a liver transplant and the first brain surgery, so at this point, his laughter and his inner eagerness to just get the surgery over with told me he was again positive about the outcome. This time his family was not there to be with us, but my minister came. Talking to my minister made the time go faster. The nurse had told us that they would call the waiting room when surgery was over; the surgery was not as long as the first. The telephone rang about two hours into the quiet.

"Hello," I said.

The nurse stated, "Your husband's surgery is finished."

I could hear Bob yelling in the background.

"I am supposed to tell you he is standing in the middle of his hospital bed dancing," she said with a laugh.

When I got to the recovery room, Bob was laughing and handing out suckers to the recovery room nurses. He had stuck the suckers in his surgical gown pocket. He always had them in his overnight bag. He knew his mouth would be dry, and he was a smoker, so he knew this would help.

Bob went back to work after surgery; however, his ammonia levels were higher than low these days, and he was struggling with his memory.

Steve, his boss, had pulled me aside one day when I met Bob for lunch, and he asked me, "Do you see a difference in Bob's cognitive levels lately?"

He knew I would know what he meant. My behavior classes in grad school help me understand things clearer and sooner than others do, and my experience with my son's traumatic brain injury also helped. We both knew after the second surgery things had really changed. Bob's fluids were building up in his body faster now. The ammonia was controlling his body more and more. He would have more bad days than good.

It was a Sunday morning, and I was fixing breakfast for my grandson and son. I heard a knock at the apartment door. I yelled for my grandson to answer the door. I heard the voices from the kitchen; it was Bob. He was going to church with us.

I heard my grandson yell for his dad to come into the living room. "Dad, hurry up," he said.

My back was to the entrance to the kitchen. But just as I started to turn from the stove, I felt a soft touch to the back of my neck. A kiss was so gently placed on my neck. I turned slowly to catch my boyfriend's lips. However, when turning he was holding the most beautiful roses. They were red and white with baby's breath. Bob took the spatula from my hand and place the roses in my right hand. He bent to his knees at that moment; I was so overwhelmed. I really did not know what was happening. I could see my grandson and son watching as they stood behind Bob as he knelt to the floor. Nothing seemed real at that moment.

Bob's words came. "My sweet, sweet love," his words were shaky, "you know you have my heart. Will you take this ring and be my bride and wife?"

As his words came, the ring was right there staring me in the face.

Bob and I had been seeing each other for about six months. We took time out from work to play a lot. We walked each day together and fished as often as we could. We just kept looking for more and more things to enjoy. Each thread of our life had been to just take the time to share our dreams.

The ring was still there, and Bob was still on his knees. It just seemed to be the biggest thing in front of me. I took Bob's hand to try to get him to stand up to get him off his knees. My words could not surface. Time seemed to be frozen until I heard my son say, "It is okay, Mom. He loves you."

I reached down and took the ring. Bob was up off the floor putting the ring on my finger. My kids were screaming and yelling as Bob pulled me into his arms roses and all and kissed me, and his kiss was just like sweet butter that had melted from the sun on a picnic table. I pulled away from him gently to get a better look at the ring. It was silver, white gold with three diamonds. It could have been a bubble gum wrapper made into a circle. At that moment, my body seemed to change; I felt full. My strength of being seemed the strongest it had ever felt. My heart was beating so hard its beats confused me. The beats were something I knew well. They were like the rhythm I felt from the music in church—something that often filled my soul. Though just as complete.

Bob's words came quickly. "Will you marry—"

"Yes, yes," I said, and the dance began.

Bob often teased me about having running shoes on; it just always seemed more natural to run away from a committed relationship than to stay. Now he mentioned that he needed to burn all my tennis shoes, so I couldn't run away from him. Life was so good at that time. Bob stayed at the apartment. The drive was long for him from the apartment to go to work, but he wanted every moment he could to be with me. It just wasn't about how long the trip took to drive to work. It was more about the time. The time he somehow felt more than me was precious. Somehow, some way, Bob's love for life, love, and his words had gotten me to stand still long enough to say yes to our love and passion.

We both decided that the wedding would be a small church wedding. God's presence was always all around us, and we both felt that and knew that in our hearts. Money was something neither of us had, but with my knowledge of local reseller shops and the help of others, I knew we could have a wedding we would be proud to share with others and call ours. My church sister lived behind me, and I ran over to her home in my housecoat. I wanted her to be the first one to see my ring and hear the news—before my church family got to see my ring. After my church sister's hugs and kisses, she asked, "Did you set a date?"

"Soon," I said, "as soon as we see when our minister could marry us."

We all got ready for church, and it did not matter what I was wearing; my outfit today was glowing.

Our first day of being engaged was beautiful. The smile on Bob face as each person shook his hand at church was enough for me to know his love was real and true. I knew that whatever life had for us, we could take it on one day at a time. God gave us each other, and now we could share our broken pieces together. We decided on October 16, 2010, for a wedding date. He gave me five months to plan our wedding.

The search was on for that perfect wedding dress. Time was never in our favor. Bob had more bad days than good ones, and it became harder for him to even drive to work. He had left for work one morning, after staying at the apartment, and he would usually call me after he got to work; however, this morning was different. He didn't call; I waited for about an hour, and I started calling his cell phone. It just kept going to voice mail. I called his work, and Steve (Bob's boss) said he hadn't arrived yet, and he had not heard from him. Now was the time to call out the guards to search for Bob. His illness was not our best friend, and God was in control of time. The phone rang just as I was about to start at the top of the list of helpers. We always knew our church family was there if we needed them, and they stood in the shadows waiting for the calls. They were not like my son or grandson, but I knew I had someone. The ringing was the sound I heard, and I picked up the phone. It was Bob.

"I'm at Mercy Hospital. I felt funny, and my head was hurting, so I came here."

I told Bob, "I will be there soon."

I called my son and picked him up to go with me. I knew Bob's truck would have to be brought home. I drove to the hospital not knowing what to expect. After talking to the doctors, I knew Bob would need to be transferred to where he could have his own team of doctors. His brain was swollen from the tumor. The doctor stated that we needed to do a procedure to release the pressure on the brain, and, again, time was not in our favor. The staff at St. Clair Hospital knew Bob from two previous visits. They were so gentle and caring for both of us. I believe from their nature and position, they just wanted Bob to get well and our wedding vows to be exchanged as much as we did. The staff often commented on how much Bob and I loved each other, and it showed in our words, glances, and smiles that we so often traded.

The doctors came in after Bob was made comfortable. They spoke with both of us about the surgery Bob needed. The chance for recovery from surgeries was about as good as having five aces in a deck of cards, or a poker hand.

Bob had survived a liver transplant and two brain surgeries, so he said to me, "Honey, this is just another dance we have to do before we can dance at our wedding. I need to give this all I have. I have an eighteen-year-old's liver inside of me, and I need to know it is safe and lives on."

Bob seems to always have the words to ground my heart and allow me to let go of my fears and let God work his miracles. I kissed his forehead, and my eyes told him it would be okay, and I supported his decision. I had no choice; fear always lay dormant inside of me. Fear always filled my soul, but I never showed it, and somehow our love was our hope even though we had not said our vows. The nurse announced that the surgery would be in the morning. I needed to make some calls, including to Bob's mom. Bob and I always went it alone when he needed to go to the hospital, but I made the calls. Bob had always asked me to call his dad. Bob's mom and dad had been divorced for several years. After many years of Bob being separated from his dad, they had become best friends. His dad was a very kind man. When I called him he said, "I will be there with you both."

Bob was prepped for surgery the next morning, and no one was there yet. I watched as the nurses wheeled him down to the surgery. I held his warm hand, and our eyes never left each other. The doors opened, and I kissed him on his forehead. When Bob's immune system was low, I always kissed him on the forehead.

He squeezed my hand and said, "Remember our dance."

I knew that he meant our dance of life. The life dance we chose to hold onto until we could dance at our wedding. My legs were shaking as always. I knew it could be the last smile on his face I would ever see. But I knew Bob was more than just a fighter. He was a survivor. He had to have the strength of a mustard seed and the faith of many prayers that were unspoken. I let go of Bob's hand, and the nurse grabbed me as I turned. My feet just wouldn't turn me in the right direction. I asked where the chapel was, and she walked me there. She offered to sit with me, but I needed only to feel the presence of God. I prayed; I talked out loud, and I cried. I knew I had to let go and let God have him and to trust the doctors. Several hours went by with no calls from Bob's family. My son called several times. He would have been there with me, but Bob's trips to the hospitals were so many. I had learned to trust and to do it by myself. My family was a call away. Bob had given me an extraordinary gift—the promise to be my husband—and no surgery or illness was going to take that away. We both knew our future was just beneath hope, and we both had to be fighters through it all.

I wasn't around when Bob had his liver surgery; he was such a private person. We did stay in touch by phone; I could relate to his mother's pain. She was there for him, and she nurtured him back to health. The pain she felt going through almost losing a son was what I measured as my own when my son was in a car wreck, and I almost had to let him go. Maybe that is why Tim and Bob, his future stepfather, were so close. They also both had a love for fishing.

Several hours seemed to pass. I had gone to the waiting room where the sun was shining through the window. It reminded me of God's presence and that he had given us both brighter days.

I heard the voice from the pager call, "Mrs. Miller, return to room 523, please."

No thoughts were in my mind at this time except I knew I had to carry strength back with me. I entered the private room, and Bob was taped to machines; he was not awake, and the nurses were trying to make him comfortable.

"The doctor will be in to talk with you in a few moments," one nurse said.

"He was a trooper," the other nurse said. Bob had tubes taped to his shaved head, and blood was running into a jar next to him.

"He is okay." the other nurse in the room reassured me. "It is just drainage from his wound."

The doctor appeared in the room just as the nurses tucked the covers tightly under Bob's feet. His feet were always cold. We would touch our feet together when we were in bed at night, and I would say, "Warm my feet for me." Just to think of his touch still fills my body with warmth like warm water seems to fill my body with the fluids of our love.

The doctor approached me, and he said, "All went well; we took what we could of the mass. We just have to let time be our friend and watch him. We will make him and you as comfortable as we can."

They had Bob in a private room, and there was an accommodation for me in his room just steps away.

"The next hours will be critical," I heard the doctor caution.

The doctor and the nurses left the room, and I stepped out into the hallway to call my son. I never took my eyes off Bob. Suddenly I could see that the tube that was in Bob's head was no longer catching the blood. There was blood all over the floor.

I dropped the phone and started screaming for the nurse. "Help, help, please help him."

Nurses started running from all directions, and I could barely hear the code blue call announcement for my Bob's room. They whirled his bed down the hallway, and I ran with them.

A nurse stopped, grabbed me, and said, "Let go, and let them have him; it will be all right."

The nurse left my side and moved through the doors as the doors swayed back and forth. I could still hear the echoes of my screams in the hallway after me screaming again at the top of my lungs, "Please, God don't take him," but there was a warm feeling half full that I knew so well. I knew I was standing just beneath hope. I rung my hands together praying as hard as I could pacing up and down the hall. The hall seemed narrow, and the lights peered over me like fog over a rusty old bridge in the still of a cold morning. I slowly walked back to the room not knowing where to go. As I reach the door of my husband's hospital room, I could see the blood left on the floor. The blood covered the space were Bob's bed was once positioned.

I heard a soft scream in the hall. "Don't go in there."

But it was too late. The nurse reached me, and her arms were open surrounding my body.

"Come on," she said. "I will take you to a waiting room." I wanted to ask if he was alive, but I knew she couldn't tell me. That would be up to the doctors.

"I'm sorry." The nurse still was holding me as she walked me to the room.

"We did not mean to leave you alone in the hallway. We just needed to get him to help fast. Code blues aren't the sounds—words—we want the family to hear; nor do we want to leave family behind to wait out the outcome by themselves."

I was by myself, I thought.

They say that the caregiver sometimes dies before his or her family member. The caregiver just has a heart attack from being exhausted, or the stress builds up, and the person does not know how to take care of himself or herself. However, I had put some help in place. I knew some of the things would overwhelm me if I did not ask for help. Bob's family always said to call them, but they could never come. The nurse walked into the room to tell me someone would come out in just a little while to speak to me about Bob.

Bob and I knew the chances we took to remove the mass on Bob's brain. He was on blood thinners because of his liver and other medications. His white blood count was always messed up, and he had his blood drawn once a month to keep things under control.

The door swirled hard like the customer slamming the door, or a server had messed up a meal, and the patron had sent the dinner back after waiting too long to be served the second one.

The nurse appeared with the doctor. "We have him stabilized for the moment. We were afraid of this," the doctor continued. "They will bring him back to his room in a few minutes."

Just as the doctor finished his words, the doors opened again, and Bob was being wheeled off the elevator.

I met the bed as it was wheeled back to the place it once occupied. Bob was awake and talking. I held back my tears when he reached for my hand. His words came slowly.

"Where did you go?" he asked.

I knew his ammonia levels were starting to build up, and his thoughts would become cloudier.

"I didn't go anywhere, honey," I answered. "I was just waiting for you to come back from your stroll with those beautiful nurses."

His hand was so warm to the touch, and I squeezed it as he looked at me. His words were soft and weak.

He said, "You're the most beautiful woman to me and soon to be my wife." Bob's eyes were always bright and blue. The love we shared automatically came through his eyes. I could never doubt his passion when his eyes spoke to me with tenderness.

The nurses finished attending to him, and Bob and I

tucked into the darkening night for a clean start. I knew the night would be darker than most nights. I wondered how many times I would have to ring the alarm. It was surprising, but Bob slept well. He still had the tube running from his head to the jar of leftover blood. There was some blood on the floor, but most of it the nurses wiped up in the shuffle the previous night.

He had a good night; he slept as well as he could. I, on the other hand, never shut my eyes except to pray for Bob's safekeeping through the night. God had granted us his safety one more time.

His words came from a small bundle in the oversized bed. "How did you sleep?"

"Fine," I answered.

The bed I had slept in was a couch/chair that folded out into a bed. The leather seemed to seep cold through my sheets. I wanted to snuggle beside Bob, but I knew I would wake him. I knew Bob would have loved the company. We always tried to bend a few rules when he was in the hospital. I remember one time we both fell asleep together in the hospital bed, and when the doctor came in the next morning, he chuckled and said, "Well, who is my patient this morning?"

We liked getting caught in the fun we had. Bob and I both shared the love for fun in a life full of do and don'ts. Our love spoke without words.

The nurse had joined us now, and she said, "Well, I heard from a little birdy you two got caught snuggling, right?"

Bob answered, "Well, if you would give us more privacy, we would not have to bend the rules."

The nurse said, "Well, we can fix that, but somehow, I don't think it would matter to you two lovebirds."

What is it with younger people? They think because we are older, we are on our way to the old-timer's farm. I truly think the younger generations believe that aging love cannot be as strong and free as young love. Love was, is, to Bob and me, young and full of breath. Young breath in our old bodies!

Fishing was an art for Bob; he knew just the right bait to put on the end of a line. He had so many fishing poles that I wondered how the man had money to eat when he was living by himself. I would sit in the boat watching him cast, and the dramatic moves were like the dance of a performer at a ballet. For the most part, Bob believed in catch and release, unless it was a special trophy. It was for the most part catch and release. My son, Tim, loved fishing with Bob. They had so much in common.

I spent several days with Bob in the hospital. Several days by his side and only when the nurse cautioned me to take some time for myself did I do so; I always felt it was not about me. It was about us getting to the altar to give our love to each other and letting the world know what that love was all about. I made a promise to Bob when I took his engagement ring, and I was going to honor him any way I could.

It was touch and go for a while, but Bob was finally released from the hospital. Bob was not going to allow his recovery to get in the way of our wedding. We had to get the announcements out, and I knew he could work on them while he was recovering at home.

We had chosen something simple. I found some unopened blank invitations at a local thrift store. It was my go-to for things, as well as the other reseller stores. The invitations had a raised circle on the inside. Bob and I had decided to scan our baby pictures, from when we were both around the age of three. We downloaded them and put them in the circle, and the blank card now read, "Guess who is getting married." Bob and I liked simple things and to have fun with life. We let our inner child have fun a lot.

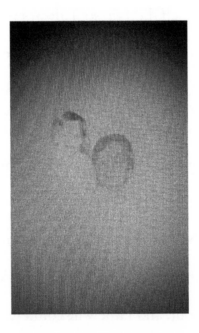

This picture was on our wedding invitations.

It read, "Guess who is getting married."

The preparation for the wedding was like a scavenger hunt. I needed to get my wedding dress, and Bob wanted a big church wedding. Someone told me about a wedding store or bridal shop in St. James, Missouri. The owner appeared to be a Christian woman and down to earth. The shop featured new and used wedding gowns. My church sister went with me to check out what the shop housed. The shop was small, and there were samples of new things and used. Some of the things had to be ordered. There was a rack in the corner of the room with dresses. They were marked down. My kind of shopping. There, tucked in the middle of the rack, was an ivory and beige bridal dress. I looked at the price tag; it had one price marked through, and it read $2,400. Then it had another price marked through, $1,200; the price that remained was $198.

I quickly asked as I showed the owner the dress and the tag, "What is wrong with this dress?"

The woman explained. "Someone had ordered it and had it altered and then never picked it up."

It was a size twelve. I looked at my church sister, and she said, "Try it on; you never know. I hurried to the dressing room, and, sure enough, the dress seemed to fit. I pulled the dressing room curtains open and came out, and all eyes were on me.

Donna, my church sister, said, "Step to the mirror."

I could not believe my eyes. It was perfect! It had beige embroidery all over the dress. Ivory was the main color. I turn from the mirror, and my church sister started snapping pictures. "I feel like a princess," I said. Bob would always call me his princes and now I believed him, and my head was swirling with thoughts.

Bob was doing well with the surgery. He always seems to come back fighting. As I stood beside his bed, I looked at him with love pounding in my heart. He was the man I would marry. The love of a new life. As my thoughts continued, familiar voices came from the hallway. I stepped to the hospital room door, and, sure enough, it was Gary and Barb. "Hey, guys, what you are doing here?" I asked. Gary answered, "Mom is in the next unit; she had a stroke, and we brought her here." I began to tell them that Bob was in for brain surgery and that he had been in a car wreck.

Barb said, "You look tired."

I answered, "I am. Bob has been in here two days now, and I have not been home. I can't sleep in the hospital.

"Let's go down to the waiting room," Barb said. "Maybe what you need is some sunlight!"

Barb and Gary were friends from the Elks. I moved there in 2007 and met them when I joined the Elks. They were excellent people. Gary was like a brother to me and Bob.

Bob had been sleeping when I left the room, but when we returned he was awake. I introduced Bob to them, and we all started talking about when I lived in Washington and how I needed to move back. We told them Bob and I were getting married, and we would need a place to live. Gary said they might have the perfect location for us. So before they left, they gave us a number to call, and Gary told me to drive by and look at it and to let them know. Bob had a bass boat, lots of tools, a canoe, and lots of fishing gear. We needed a house with a garage and space.

We stayed ten more days in the hospital. Each day, Bob got back to himself. When the nurses came into Bob's room, he was always bragging about how I was his princess, and our wedding was going to be the best. Bob would tease me about how he took my running shoes away from me. Anytime I would get too close to a relationship, I would run. I had been married before, and the marriage lasted twenty-six years. I had two handsome sons. Bob had two daughters and had been married twice, once when he was very young, and he went off to the army. Soon after his first marriage his wife introduced, she was going to have a baby, Bob said it was a good time in his life. Bob had the softest heart—a child's heart—but the wisdom of a man full of love.

Bob came from a family of one brother and four sisters. He had one sister that died in a car accident. His family never seemed to recover from her death. Bob's Mom had a huge picture painted of her daughter, and it hung over the fireplace.

His mom had the kind of love and control over her children that I did not understand. I wondered if our marriage would work because of her control. She would tell me stories about her husband, Robert, Bob's dad. As Bob became older and wiser, he realized what was going on, and he wanted to stay in touch with his dad. Bob's dad was a wonderful man. He was full of love and compassion. The memories he shared showed how much he loved his children. But Bob was the only one with whom he would stay in touch. I could see where Bob got his love of life. Bob's stepmother had died ten years before Bob and I got together. Ann was German through and through. She also was a wonderful person. I met her several years before she died.

Two more days passed, and Bob was released from the hospital. He could not wait to get back to work. He was a drug and alcohol counselor. The wedding plans were on again. Bob got word his dad was ill, and Bob wanted him to be his best man. So we would choose a date when we knew he could attend. Also, we had to check with our preacher/

minister on dates and if the church would be available. That was my only request. I knew if my first marriage lasted for twenty-six years, God had to be on our side and walking with us. Bob wanted to take care of all the guys' suits or tuxes, and when he knew the color of my dress, he knew he wanted the color for the guys' tuxes to be beige, so the color in my dress would match. Now to pick out a color for the dresses for the bridesmaids. We chose burgundy.

Bob was getting stronger every day from the surgery, but the operation itself had taken more life from him. I met him at his workplace one day, and his boss, Steve pulled me aside and asked me if I had seen a difference in Bob after the surgery. He went on to say that Bob could not remember as well as he once did. His thoughts were getting harder to receive. I was afraid of this. Bob's cognitive ability was just not there. The chemicals in his body were becoming more and more unstable. His ammonia levels were out of control. When I first learned how this could happen to his liver, I just took a step back to think about what we were doing getting married, while neither of us knew what Bob's health would bring to our lives.

Bob thought he would surprise me and take the day off early to spend some special time with me. After Bob's health changed, we knew time together was a gift.

I was retired, and for the most part I was home all the time. I could tell this day was not really meant to be a surprise. His liver was acting up. Bob and I lived together. He had moved in with me and my son and grandson. My son was between jobs, and he was staying with me to save money.

He wanted all of us to go swimming. We had a pool at the apartment complex. So we spent the day swimming and talking and spending some much-needed time together as a couple and as a family. It wasn't until Bob was sitting on the front porch that my son came into the house to tell me that Bob didn't seem to be himself. He went on to state that Bob was acting confused. I went out to check for myself, and I came to the same conclusion. Bob's liver was acting up. I asked him if he felt all right, and he could barely get his words to come out of his mouth. I called my son to help me get Bob inside. By this time Bob could not walk. I got Bob's contact information and called Barnes Hospital. They said to bring him in. I lived in Sullivan at the time, which was over a hundred miles away, so I knew that was out of the question. Bob seemed to be dying right before my eyes. I could tell this day was not really meant to be a surprise. His liver was acting up.

"Bob, I said, "we have to get you to the hospital. Tim, my son, and I will take you."

"I don't know," Bob said.

By this time, he did not know where he was or who we were. I gathered up all his medications and all his contacts. My son helped me get him in the car. Bob was now in the phase of someone drunk—very drunk. It was all we both could do to get him to the hospital. Bob had a team of doctors that always had to be called. One could not make a decision without the other one. Panic mode was always lurking inside of me, but urgency for me to do something to help always seems to way over it. I just knew I had to be strong for both of us. The doctors all checked him over, and, as we suspected, Bob's brain surgery had taken just enough out of him to cause his liver to flare up. So now the doctors would have to keep him in the hospital. The chemicals in his body needed to balance out. His fluids had to be drained from his liver. The procedure would be to put a long needle in his stomach and drain the fluids. They would have to be very cautious not to touch the liver. Bob was in and out; one minute he knew me, and the next he didn't know where he was. Several hours passed, and I told my son to go home. He could take my car and go. My grandson was staying with a sister from church who lived in the same apartment complex. I didn't want my son to see Bob like this anymore. I wanted him to remember the fishing trips they took together.

"Go on, Son; go home and take care of Blaine." I was pleading with him at this point.

Tim took my keys and left. All the doctors had left the room; however, they were just a page away. I crawled into the bed beside Bob. I had my Flip Flog on, so I just kidded them off and put my feet under the covers; his feet were warm like sand on a warm, sunny day. We both loved the sand; ocean and any kind of water you could give us we would take. I kissed Bob on the cheek, and his skin was salty and clammy. Maybe I just thought he would come back to me if we could touch. Our church was in my thoughts and the many prayers the people had shared. I needed the thoughts for energy. I also needed to know what to expect from Bob's relapse. Then the words slipped from Bob's lips.

"You want to get naked and get under the covers with me?" Bob was always trying to joke and get me off guard to forget about what was going on. Bob's cognitive ability was coming back almost as fast as it had disappeared. I took my fingers and touched his lips as I motioned him a kiss. His body was broken like a walking stick but as tender as a baby.

Our love for each other was like the sands of time. It just gave us one small pebble of life at the moment we needed. We knew time could not be on our side. But Bob wanted our wedding to seal the clock of pain we had both experienced and to show the world we had overcome our struggles once again. Our love was just that strong. People go through life never holding onto time, but time had to be our best friend, and we didn't want to lose a minute.

The nurse appeared in the doorway and caught us together in bed. When I started to get up, she said, "Oh, no, honey, just stay right there! That is the best medicine for him. It looks like it is already working." Bob would have to stay overnight, and my son would come to get us in the morning.

From that day on, I knew I would be on a roller coaster with Bob's health, but what better way to love someone than on a roller coaster, high in the air and never coming down— with both of us almost reaching for the stars and trying to get a glimpse of heaven. Bob knew he could not go back to work. He loved his job. I had lunch with him one day at his work. Bob had a couch in his office. It was more like a love seat. I sat down on it, and I don't know what came over me, but I put my feet up over the armrest of the love seat.

I said, "I bet you never had your girlfriend on your couch like this before." Just as I finished my words, Bob's boss walked to the doorway.

I started to sit up, but he said, "Don't bother, but if you two need to close the door, it doesn't bother me." We both laughed. Most of the staff would drop by Bob's office to steal Hershey chocolate kisses from the oversized candy kiss music box I gave Bob.

He said, "Thanks. I just wanted to spread some love around."

On his way out of the room, he said to Bob, "Where did you find her, and do they have more?"

That was Bob's last days to work. We did not know that at the time, but he only went back to clean out his office. My son and I went with him. It was a somber day for Bob. Through his struggle with his liver, he wanted to go back to work after he had mended. He gave it three good years.

It was one more bridge we crossed together. Bob appeared

after that day to counsel everyone. He just could not seem to get past the day he closed out his office—or the loss.

He fished more now. That was his second love. His job was his first. Now he would kid with me that I had moved up the ladder, and I was at the top now. Bob's blue eyes always seemed to pour out words that never needed to be said, although he told them often.

The words seemed to suck us in like we were breathing in the ghost. It was a rebirth of love for the both of us. When I was in high school, our art teacher asked us to define love. I often go back to the struggle I had that day to describe it. How can you explain something like love or even trace it out at sixteen or seventeen? But now, after many years of trial and error, I see love as a choice—a choice to love and to let yourself feel and let go of anything stopping choice. But the way you choose to be passionate is what two people have to give to each other. We did not have a lot of money. I had my retirement money, and Bob had no money, but he was a man that held onto life in so many ways. We flew kites together;

we took off our shoes in the middle of the park and walked in the grass alongside each other; we fished together in the rain, and we love in the middle of the day on a blanket in the park. Even though the struggles were there with Bob, we never struggled with our love.

He started yelling at me, "You bitch, I will just leave your ass." He went to get things in order to move out, but when his ammonia levels came back down, he would not remember his angry words. My love for Bob taught me to hold on tight because the road would or could get bumpier. Most people would have run, but Bob had taken my running shoes away.

The final things for the wedding were just about finished, and Bob seemed to be okay at this point—maybe just a little frail. We didn't want the typical wedding. The music we chose for me to go down the aisle was by Tim McGraw, "My Best Friend."

One of my church sisters and good friend, Norma, sang "The Rose," by Bette Midler. Bob sang a song by George Strait—"I Give My Heart."

Bob told me that we were going to go from our wedding to our reception in a hot-air balloon. He also shared with everyone that same thing. Except for his best friend and our minister, no one really knew the truth of the matter. Bob knew I was afraid of heights. Bob loved to surprise me, and he also loved to play pranks on me. Our wedding day was no different. The special day did not give me a free pass from Bob's jokes. I was just not going to get into a hot-air balloon.

Bob and I chose red roses for wedding flowers. We also had a sand ceremony; we decided white sand for purity, beige for our bodies, and burgundy for the blood of Christ. The Trinity—Father, Son, and Holy Ghost. Our wedding and our love were like the sands of time that would live on forever. Each piece of sand represented the years before our wedding and the years to come.

So much of us was being put out there before God and our family. They witnessed what our love indeed was to each other. The church was not full like our lives were that day. On one side I could see, when I took a look through the church doors before entering, Bob walking around in his beige tux, white shirt, and burgundy vest talking to people. He had told the minister he wanted to wait for some people that weren't there yet. That was Bob always taking charge, wanting everything as perfect as it could be on our special day. Looking at him through the doors, he seemed to be a very tall man, and Bob always said he was five feet nine, but when we kissed, he met my lips, and the force of his kiss was a very strong kiss. We still had that force of energy. When we touched, our bodies meshed into one.

Bob could reach for me, and what power he had would go into the most tender and loving dance of love. Our bodies just seemed to cling to the movement.

Oh, But the Dance

I gently turn to kiss the sweat from your face; my tongue slowly touches each eyelid, licking and forming a path down your nose; it finds the way to your lips. I press mine against yours, tasting the leftover pleasures we both just exchanged. The hardness of my body touches your chest, and you jerk with excitement; with one sudden movement your arm circled my waist, and the dance starts again. Slowly you move your hands down my back to rest on each cheek, and we melt together like icing to a hot cake; you shiver with delight, and with a scream the dance begins. The rhythm sets the beat to each raindrop pounding against the windowpane; harder and harder the beat was felt until the dance stirred the excitement within us—one scream after another letting the silence know it could be no more. Would it ever stop? The pleasure, oh so much pleasure, swelling inside like the tides of the ocean; higher and higher and louder and louder the voices grew. The moisture spilled from our bodies as the dance took on new meaning. The rain, the dance, and the screams wouldn't last forever? The dance became less, and the touch became tender, slowly bringing our bodies back to motionless silhouettes. As the rain slowed, exhaustion set in. Oh, but the dance. Was it a dream? Would it stay forever in the memories of our minds, hearts, and souls?

Oh, but the dance!

Now there he was, just waiting for the first dance and the dance that would guide us through the high waters of time. As I stood there, I could not see the illness in the man. I only saw the man that had a special kind of love to give, and he wanted us to share it. The minister then opened the doors to let me know the wedding was going to start. My bridesmaids were ready. My maid of honor took the roses and placed them in my hands. At that moment the heaviness of the flowers carried the weight of Bob's illness out of my heart. The doors opened, and my sons gently wrapped their arms together with mine and walked me down the aisles. When I reached the corridor that led straight to the altar, I could see Bob standing beside his father and his best friend, Jim. I lifted my head, and our eyes met. Bob's body shook back and forth, and it appeared he was going to fall. His dad reached for him. His dad held onto him, and at that moment the love of his father's strength held him up. Bob stood taller now, and his blue eyes spoke to me every step I took. I did not feel the weight my sons were carrying. But they told me and laughed about it later. When I reached the altar, my sons took my flowers and handed them off to Mary, my maid of honor. Bob took my hands and kissed me on my cheek.

He whispered, "You are my princess, and you are so beautiful. How can I ever love you with this broken body?

I knew right then he would smother me with all his passionate words, for what time he had to give us, and I knew God was on our side to provide us with time in his own way to see life, touch life, and taste life like we were young and just beginning. God would help our childlike souls and hearts stay whole and young.

The minister started the ceremony—our words shared, our hands touching—and our kiss was a witness for what seemed like thirty minutes. For thirty minutes I held him up, and I knew then there would be many more times God and I would be Bob's strength.

The wedding pictures seemed to take forever. It's then that I felt so in charge of my life. People waiting for me, us, and things seem to just stand still for a moment. Bob was outside, and everyone seemed to be gathering with him. What was he up to?

I heard the minister say," Well, Bob I brought a ladder. She should be able to climb up on the ladder to get into the balloon."

Oh no. I forgot about the hot-air balloon. He really did it. *I am going to my reception in a hot-air balloon* were my fearful thoughts. The weather was just right. It was a fall day in October. The leaves were in full color of burgundy, gold, and orange, and they would be beautiful looking down from the heavens. The clouds were sharp blue and white like the colors of Bob's eyes. When I walked through the doors, people were standing on both sides of the parking lot, and the noise, all hands seemed to be clapping. The clapping made me forget about my fear of the balloon ride. It looked like a parade was just getting ready to start. Bob met me at the door and took my hand.

He said, "Look up over there," and he pointed to the sky.

As I looked up, my legs began to buckle. Just then, I heard the whinny of a horse. A white carriage appeared from around the back of the church. It was drawn by one horse, and the driver was a woman wearing a black and white tux with a burgundy bow tie. I started crying.

Bob looked at me and said, "Nothing too good for my princess. You're going to the reception like a princess would." The reception hall was not that far, but Bob had called the police to get an escort through town, and they took us the long way around. Bob took my hand and helped me into the carriage. My son helped my granddaughter, the flower girl, onto the seat next to the driver. My grandson rode on the other side of the driver. Bob's dad and my maid of honor rode in opposite seats to us in the carriage. The carriage led the parade as my sons and family and friends followed. As we entered the highway, the police—our escort—pulled in front of us, and we were the best float in the show. I felt like I was floating on each and every one of the clouds I had seen at the church while looking up for the hot-air balloon. As we moved along, the people in the cars, bikes, and trucks were stopped along both sides of the road.

"They're here to see the princess," Bob said. "I told you that our wedding would be the life of royalty." At that moment I never felt so complete in my whole life. This day seemed just for me, but I knew it was our day, and Bob felt like a king riding with his princess. It seems like the world stopped, and I was dreaming. So many cars stopped, horns honking and people yelling. I even heard a lady, seated in her car, say to her daughter, "Isn't this the most beautiful thing you have ever seen?" My son screamed from the car behind us. "Wave, Mom. Wave at the people." I started my wave in a swirl motion, and my maid of honor said to me, "No, like this. Wave like a princess." She cupped her hand and motioned. The ride seemed to be forever, just like the love in our hearts. We reached the church, and some of the people were already there. They helped us down from the carriage. Bob had iced a bucket of white wine, and we had a toast while we were being carried to the church. Bob's dad had toasted a piece of bread and put it in a box just the right size. As Bob made the toast, his words came softly and gently out of his mouth. "I hope this is only a small part of the love and respect I can show you the rest of my life." Bob's dad reached for his handkerchief to wipe the tears from his eyes.

Bob and I believed life was much more precious to us. We were not young, and we already had a battle in front of us to win, and we knew our armor was not new. It had been rusted from the battles before our marriage. We entered the hall, and everything was just perfect. A touch of fall was seen on the tables. The candy dishes with full of fall-colored M&Ms. A bottle of sparkling grape juice was on each table. The cake was beautiful. My grandmother's buttercream icing was used for the three-layer cake. Fresh red roses were placed just right on each side of the cake. It felt just like I was dreaming and sleepwalking. I could tell by Bob's grip on my hand that I was holding him up for a small moment. I just did not know that the grip would be longer than a moment. Bob was tired, and it showed not just with me but to everyone. Well, we had the hall for two hours. I knew the excitement would wear us both down.

One day when my church sister and I were shopping before the wedding, Bob surprised us and met us at the resale shop. We had finished our shopping, and Bob had wandered off looking. I went to find him because we were ready to leave, and, of course, he was in the toys. There in the middle of all the toys was Bob riding on a large children's rocking horse. His inner child had come out to play.

Bob said, "You can get me this for a wedding present."

We had the best laugh. He was so entertaining. I told my church sister what he said, and I told her I had an idea. I was going to come back and get the horse for the wedding. My thoughts were that when Bob and I would throw the flowers and garter at the wedding, I would, along with my bridesmaid and maid of honor, bring in the horse as a surprise. It wasn't easy for me to surprise Bob; he was always one step ahead of me. I had my bridesmaids meet me in the ladies' restroom. There sat the horse. I gave them all cowboy hats and told them my son was going to play the song "These Boots Are Made for Walking" as I pulled the horse out onto the floor

They knew what to do—just act funny and have fun with it. When we entered the hall with the horse and our cowboy hats, I handed Bob his cowboy hat, and the guests went wild. I danced around the horse pulling my dress up to show off the cowboy boots; I had borrowed the boots from Bob's mother. Bob's eyes were so big. He played right along. He climbed on the horse and started rocking like a child. His body was so small-framed. I danced around him, and he just played along. The guests loved it. After the music stopped, Bob just yelled "hee haw" and waved his hat in the air. He appeared to have the time of his life. All his sickness was left behind at that moment. My thoughts were, *There is no laughter in time unless we fill time with laughter.* But Bob was all about laughter. He would or could find ways to make me laugh.

He kissed me after he got off the horse and said, "Honey, now this was my carriage ride." Our words always seemed so poetic together. He filled me up when I was empty, and the laughter he shared became fuel for my heart and soul.

We took the money from the wedding and drove to

Venice, Florida. We spent a week with my girlfriend Gale and then made it on to Key West. Bob had lived there for a while, and he wanted me to see the end of the earth and the paradise. Our honeymoon was a step back in time for Bob. I felt he was retracing his steps backward for a reason. The trip wore him down, and he was exhausted. We had to ask my girlfriend to go along. I think back now, and I believe Bob was always afraid of death at his door. I suppose I asked Gale to go with us so I would have someone to hold onto if anything happened to him. His struggle to travel back to his past was pulling the life out of him.

The trip was so hard on him; his ammonia levels were high, and Bob had soiled his shorts, and he did not even recognize what was going on. When I asked him if I could help him, he acted and talked like a drunken man. But Bob's will to be on that island was overwhelming and was evident to Gale and me. We finished the day, and Bob fell asleep when we got back to the hotel room.

Gale asked me to step outside so we could talk.

She said, "I am concerned about Bob being sick and how you are going to take care of him."

"I will figure it out, Gale; our love will have to be our strength. He gives me happy moments that words can't express; I want to love him with all I have."

As Bob would say, "Each memory of our love is the strength I need to get well."

Our trip home was a struggle. Bob took several days and weeks to get strong again. Bob seemed to be close to our minister. He even volunteered to do some work at the church. When Bob got stronger, he and Tim would work in the church. I didn't want Bob going alone. He was stronger, but his strength was measured by the need to stay active.

One day he came in from fishing and said, "Let's go look at a house in Washington your friends told us about. We need something bigger for all our stuff."

Bob had not moved his things in yet, and he had a lot of tools and fishing gear. We took the day and drove up to Washington. We called our friends, Gary and Barb. They told us to look at the house first, and they would meet us later. The house was in an excellent location. I loved the surroundings. It was like being in the country but yet in the city. A red barn was next door. It reminded me of my childhood and living on a farm. The house had a little bit of land with the town at our back door. We looked through the windows; the house still had lots of stuff in it. Not furniture but lots of boxes. We could both see the house needed a lot of work inside. It had been sitting empty for two years or more. It had a garage and a shed out back. There seemed to be lots of room for all our stuff. As I stated before, the house needed lots of work. Bob said it would take time just for us to live in it. Our questions were what would it cost, and who would pay for it? Barb and Gary pulled up just as we were walking away from the house. We stopped and talked.

Gary said, "If you guys want to do the work, we will buy the stuff you need as you go."

Questions came fast, and thoughts were, *What if Bob doesn't have the strength he needs to do massive things?* We really had to think about this. We talked to the family and friends, and we moved in in April 2011; well, we got the house in April and started the work. All the carpets needed to come out, and the doors and frames had to be replaced—lots and lots of work. We worked a couple of days, and then Bob needed rest. He wanted so much to give me a home. This was the only way we could have the place we needed and the only way we could afford it.

We had gotten enough work done that we could actually move in. Although it wasn't the cleanest place, we were moved in for the long haul. Mice had overrun the site in the two years that it had sat empty. My son could not believe I had moved in with all the mice. He knew how OCD I was about being clean. I just knew it would be a fight or race to see who slept in the bed—the mice or Bob and I. He teased me that he could set traps all around the bed. The laughter we shared was so good for us.

We worked all summer on the house, between Bob getting down sick for a few days and then back to work again. He always seems to come back to me but a little less of what he was.

One night he ate ice cream before he went to bed. He said it upset his stomach a little. I knew Bob's ammonia levels were up again because he was putting on weight. His stomach looked like he was four months pregnant. I always knew that when Bob put on weight, it could be one step away from a trip to the hospital. Bob's stomach would always build up fluids. It was a very restless night; he had taken on a cold. I heard him in the middle of the night get up to go to the bathroom. When he came back to the bed, I asked him what was wrong.

He said again, "My stomach is upset." I listened to him toss and turn for several hours. But I fell back to sleep. I always was a light sleeper and could hear Bob or feel his movement in the bed. I heard him coughing again, but this time it was a cough like he was throwing up. I ask him if he was all right,

He said, "I am throwing up the ice cream I ate."

I brought him a dishpan from the bathroom and a cold

washcloth. Then the cough came again. It went all over the bed. He tried to hit the bucket, but it went all over the walls and on the carpet. Concerned, I looked closer. I could see it was brown, but it was mixed with a lot of blood. He could not stop throwing up. I knew now it was his liver again. I put Bob in the shower and called for an ambulance. I changed his clothes and waited. The ambulance arrived, and I followed them to the hospital in my car. They took him to the trauma center at Barnes Jewish Hospital. The local hospital was not set up for this kind of trauma. The trauma center was in the basement of the hospital. It appeared to be some kind of procedure room. I watched as they hooked Bob up to all the machines. He was still throwing up. They worked with him for what seemed to be hours. Then a buzzer would go off, and they would all run out of Bob's room down the hall. They left Bob alone, and he kept throwing up blood all over the floor. There was a drain in the bare concert floor that reminded me of a basement drain. The blood ran everywhere, and I watched helplessly. I watched his machines go off, and no one came. I watched a man die across the hall, and they came to pull the curtains. I started pacing up and down the hallway. I went to the nurses' station and the desk several times to get help. How could Bob survive? He was small, and there was so much blood. As I hurried down the hall one more time, I passed a tall, thin man standing next to the hall wall. He seemed to be of a different culture. He had dark skin with coal black hair. He wore a tan suit, white shirt and tie, and he positioned himself against the wall with his hands intertwined together. When I passed him this time, he stopped me with his words. He never introduced himself, but his words came with strength.

"You have to fight for him, ma'am. He can't fight for himself right now. His heart is not going to be strong enough for all this trauma." I called for a nurse from the spot I stood. She came, and we got into an argument about what I could see; his heart rate was fifty-one. Bob was awake through all of the trauma. I just watched my husband squirm from the top to the bottom of the bed like a mouse. I knew someone had to do something.

The voice came again from the man standing against the wall.

"Then fight," he said. "Fight for him."

I ran down the hallway and demanded they do something. I was told the team they needed to use was backed up with work on the other floor.

I yelled, "Call the head guy."

They picked up the phone and made the call.

I screamed over the phone to him. "Get me some help for my husband."

He told me the same thing the nurses had been telling me; they would get to him as soon as they could. I ran up and down, and my only support was a man against the wall and God.

The man spoke again "Don't stop now," he said. "Keep pledging for him."

I felt like a mouse caught in a trap, helpless.

The man said, "Your husband cannot talk for himself. You have to be strong. He needs you as his advocate. Keep fighting and pray. Pray with all your heart but ask him nothing, and he will give you all the strength you need."

I backed myself against the wall and prayed. When I lifted my head, the man in the tan suit was gone. The team had arrived, and they were calling out my name. "Mrs. Stemmler."

The doctor spoke. "We will have to cauterize your husband's blood vessels in his chest and throat; he has thrown up so hard that they have ruptured. We see this all the time on liver patients. We're sorry for your wait. Your husband is throwing up the fluids that have built up. We will be back," she said. The doctor started to leave the room. I said, "Where are you going?"

She said, "They paged me to come down here to explain to you what is going on."

"Well, that's not good enough. You need to get a team here now!"

She turned and looked at me and said okay and then

finished walking out of the room. There was so much blood. How could one person weighing only 135 pounds or less have so much blood! I took the time to use their phone to call my landlord and good friends. I didn't want to go back into the house and see all the blood. They said they would go down to the house and clean up the mess.

They did the procedure on Bob, but they explained to me that it was not going to hold and that he would have many more of these episodes. It is to be expected when the liver can't do all the work.

I changed that day. I knew now that I would have to be the one—the fighter and Bob's voice. He just did not have the strength. It would take all of our strength and prayers for God and me to get Bob home. The procedure was over now. They would move Bob to a real room. It was just a waiting game now. I felt exhaustion move into my body. I know it had been waiting for my adrenaline levels to drop to normal. I now thought about the man in the tan suit. Who was he? I wanted to thank him for his words of strength and encouragement.

Bob was sleeping, so I walked out into the hallway to look for the tall man, but he was nowhere to be found. I asked all the nurses in the hall, but no one had seen him, and no one knew him. He had saved my life and my husband's life by keeping my thoughts going in the right direction. I had to fight for Bob's life; I had to take on more courage than I had ever known. I went back to the holding room where they had moved Bob before. It was a holding room to wait for them to take him to his room. All the fight had not left me yet. I insisted they move him from the holding room to his room as soon as possible. He just needed to settle and rest. I could hear the gurgle of the leftover blood still running down the drain.

The nurse entered the room and said, "It will be awhile. Why don't you get something to eat and a cup of coffee?"

It had been awhile since I had eaten or drank anything. It was almost light outside, and we had came to the hospital in the middle of the night. I wish Bob could have seen the light of day. But he had made it, and he was still with me.

The nurse brushed by me again and said, "Bob will be

moved to …" Her words bounced a room number off my ears, but the echo of the exhaustion kept me from hearing. I had to ask her to repeat her words. I needed a coffee; no, I needed sleep. I just had to get myself prepared for the trip home. Bob was moved to a room. The coffee would give me just enough energy to get home. I had not contacted anyone. There was never enough time. I would go home and sleep and go back to the hospital.

Bob was in good hands, and he needed me to be awake and alert to all he had to say and share. I don't know how I got home except with the help and strength of God. I dropped my things on the table and went straight for the shower. *Oh, the shower*, I thought. *The shower was full of blood.* Now I would have to relive the night before. As I pulled back the shower curtains, blood was everywhere. Gary and Barb did not know there was more trauma in the shower. I jumped back at the sight. I moved with caution to the closet for a trash bag. My thoughts started. *Put the clothes in the trash bag; wash the blood down the drain, and spray off the wall.*

I could hardly lift my legs over the tub to get into the shower. As water ran over my body, it ached from exhaustion. The tears swelled as the water tried to warm my body. The warmth of the water forced the chills away. My body felt limp. I cried and cried; the emotions were so strong. I just couldn't be strong at this moment. Sleep did not come that night, nor did it come the next night. I just couldn't bring my body to a complete rest. I knew Bob would be released in the next day are two. I also knew I needed to meet with the social worker and put home care in place. I still had to work to pay for all of our expenses. Bob's money went for his personal bills.

My work already knew the outcome of what time it would take to get Bob help and be back to work. The strange thing about a long-term illness is that the spouse of the family is the long-term caretaker, but you have to work, eat, sleep, and be that caretaker. Bob's family was always aware of the big picture.

Bob never stayed in the hospital more than a couple of days now. There just wasn't anymore they could do for him.

Bob always seemed to pop back, just a little less of his strength than before. In the next few days, Bob came home. We had made sure his living will was in place, and all the care was in place for home. Although, we both knew when I went back to work that Bob would have to do his part to get back to a healthy life. He held onto hope because it had become his best friend.

Bob had been through a liver transplant seven or eight years before we were married, and he told me if he could overcome that, it was all good from here on. Sometimes I felt he was selfish because he would do just what the doctors told him not to do. I felt that out of respect and love for life and for me he would be more cautious, but not Bob.

The fishing trips became fewer with the boat because it was hard for him to take the boat out by himself. Tim, our son, would help when he could, but the help came less. In the two and half years of our marriage, Bob had three brain surgeries and several outbreaks with his liver, but this last one pulled him down more. Bob took on a cough. He was a smoker, but this was a different kind of cough. When he would lie down at night, he could not breathe. Our sleep became less, and my caring for him and working was exhausting. The visiting nurse would always leave after Bob got somewhat better. Now they just fixed his medicines twice week and checked vitals. I was off work a lot more, but I needed to work to support us. Bob knew this, but I always felt guilty leaving him. I did all the finances, grocery shopping, and housecleaning, with laundry there also. It was hard for me to be away twelve hours a day as a teacher for a private state school, and in some ways it exhausted me, but exhaustion became my strength to do it all. Yes, there were some days I wanted to run away from it all, but love, God, and hope kept me holding on. I hated my husband's illness and disease, but I loved my husband dearly. Bob just didn't seem like he was coming back as fast this time. The cough got worse, and his ammonia levels sent him back to the hospital thirteen times in the months to come. They always focused on the liver and draining the fluids off. Bob had explained the procedure. It involved a long needle going into his stomach and the fluids being drained off into a big jar. I asked to watch them do the procedure. I've lost count of how many times Bob went through the procedure. It was nothing for Bob to wear a size small one week and extra-large the next. He did not go out much during this time. He hid his illness. He was a very proud man. I just kept working caretaking and praying for God to give me some of the hope that Bob held onto. I knew that when I could get rest, I had to rest. I had to rest for the next fight for Bob's life. Everyone told me that taking care of myself was very important. But it was so very hard to balance what I needed to do with what I should be doing. Bob's cough continued to keep us up at night. I was still working my usual shifts at work—six to six. It was so hard for me to let go of Bob while I was working. I was in prayer mode most of the time. Praying he would take care of himself and rest while I was gone, and praying he would be okay till I got back. If Bob would feel a little better during the day, he would venture out or tinker in his garage. Banjo, his dog, would follow Bob where ever he would go. I am certain Banjo was a gift, and he had a gift of nurturing his master. I had bought Banjo the October before Bob died. Banjo was an anniversary present to him. I had seen cages set up at the local Petco when I was running an errand. I ventured over to take a look, and inside a portable kennel was Banjo.

He was shy, but his eyes spoke to me. He needed a permanent home. I reached in to pet him. I knew Bob would agree. Banjo would be Bob's gift for our second anniversary. There were other dogs, but none spoke to me like Banjo. I snapped a picture on my cell phone and sent it and a text to my husband. He had been having a good day, so I asked if he could come down to see if he and Banjo would bond. He agreed to join us after he questioned if we could afford him or not, and I reassured him that if he wanted the dog, I would find a way. Bob arrived soon after the text. He was still weak from his last hospital visit. I showed him Banjo and the other few dogs. Bob sat down on the sidewalk and leaned up against a pole. Banjo sat down beside him. It was a picture worth a thousand words. It was two lost souls leaning on each other. After a few moments of leaning and leaving them alone, I came back to tell Bob that Banjo was his. Happy anniversary. Banjo was coming home with us, and after that day, Banjo never left Bob's side. He was a smart dog. He didn't like Bob or me to shut any doors inside our home. Banjo told us, in his own voice, that he wanted to stay close to Bob, and he wanted to be able to get to me if Bob needed me. Banjo was not a service dog, but he was very protective. As I mentioned before, he was a very smart dog. When Bob would go out to his garage, Banjo would sit and bark at the garage door until Bob or I would let Banjo out with him.

Bob's cough continued to keep me up at night, and the need for me to sleep also exhausted me. I put myself into counseling to help me sort out all the things about Bob's illness. It was a place to go to vent about all the things Bob had been able to listen to before.

One thing the social worker at the hospital told me was, "Learn to take care of yourself."

The counselor was the first step. She would just let me ramble about all the stuff in my head and heart. The doctor had told us at Bob's last visit that the liver disease was progressing, and things over the next few months would weaken Bob to the need for a cane, a walker, and then a wheelchair. There was no denying the disease this time. No new liver and no hope for recovery. I cried at every word that came from his mouth. Bob's liver was really weak and fragile. The doctor's words overwhelmed me, but they worked just the opposite on Bob. He reached for hope again. He held onto that word, feeling like it was the wings that would carry him through each day. Sure enough, he went back into the hospital several weeks later. His ammonia levels were high again, and the fluid was pressing on his lungs. He also still had a cough. Bob had a team of doctors at Barnes Jewish Hospital. They would never visit one at a time. The team always came as a team, and they always met with me as a team. There wasn't anything about Bob's illness that was not a struggle for him. My first call was always to the doctor. He would walk me through the journey. The Sheriff's Department would be called, while I had the doctors on the phone. In Bob's situation, he would most often resist the care he needed because ammonia levels would put pressure on his brain, and this would cause him to resist the caregiver, so the police always came for extra help if needed. Banjo would guard over Bob until I gave the command for Banjo to let go. The scene was so familiar to Banjo and me, but never did it get any easier. The ambulance would take off with its sirens on and the police car right behind. Banjo would start barking after all the doors were shut. I would start praying that I would have the mind-set to drive. Banjo would crawl up on the bed and lie in Bob's spot. No matter when I returned home, Banjo was always in Bob's spot.

My mind would wander back to the things Bob held so dear. I recall that he wanted so much to have family around for Christmas. The last Christmas, 2012, Bob wanted to have a big tree, and he wanted our children to be there at our home. Homemade candy and cookies were to be baked. We only had a little tree that was always enough for me. The money was not there to spend on a tree, but I set out on a Saturday to find something that would fit our budget. Trees were not cheap. After several stores and resell shops, I thought I would try the Dollar General store. Someone had commented that they had bought a seven-foot tree there last year, and it was very nice. I was checking out the trees, and all they had left were two seven-foot Christmas trees. One was an opened original box that was somewhat soiled, and the other one had not been opened. Thinking I could take on the used tree, I asked the cashier how much it was priced.

She said, "It was left over from last year," and she would

have to take it to checkout to get the price. She scanned the box and stood there without a word.

"Let me get my manager," she said. "That can't be right."

"Well, what is the price?" I asked.

"It rang up for a penny," she continued.

Apprehensive, I thought, *What could be wrong with it?* The manager arrived and assured the cashier the price was right. It had been left over from last year and had been inventoried out for a penny. She told me they had just checked it over the day before, and it was okay. One penny for a Christmas tree. How could I have gotten so lucky? On the way home, I thought about decorating. Bob and I could combine the ones we had. Bob wanted an old-fashioned Christmas, so we could make garland out of popcorn. I could put my crocheted tablecloth around the trunk for a tree skirt. We would call it our penny tree. The tree cost only a penny and no taxes, but it was the prettiest tree ever. Bob took joy in telling the story about our old-fashioned Christmas and our penny tree. God had worked his magic once again with our budget.

Our children and grandchildren shared the memories of our last Christmas together with their stepfather and step-grandfather. Somehow *step* never was part of Bob's vocabulary in life. He touched their lives as a father and grandfather should. Bob was all about memories, and he tried very hard to leave everyone with the purest.

Starr was the youngest grandchild, and she still tears up when she sees the tree.

Every time she says, "I'm still mad at Grandpa because he left before he took me fishing."

Bob loved to fish; besides his job as a drug and alcohol counselor, it was his love in life. He had enough fishing rods for every angel in heaven.

God worked his magic again that day. The kids still talk about the memories of that Christmas—the abundance of cookies and candy and love.

Our road to recovery was not over; Bob continued to have a cough. It was just a dry cough at first, but I cautioned him that he needed to get it checked out when he had his checkup in January 2013. Of course, when the time came, I took off work and took Bob to his appointment. The doctor was almost finished with examining Bob when he asked if there was anything else Bob wanted to talk about.

Bob said no.

But I looked at him, and he changed his answer.

Well, Doctor, my wife wants me to tell you about this dry cough I have acquired." Right away the doctor called down to set up a procedure to have Bob's lungs checked. I went into the exam room with Bob; as they scoped Bob's lungs, pieces of a mass started floating away from the walls of his lungs. They stopped the exam right away and explained to Bob that he would have to come back in March to see a lung specialist.

They went on further to explain that he would have to be completely sedated for the exam. This was not good. With all the things wrong with Bob, the doctors never wanted him fully sedated. The hospital would not let us leave until we had the appointment scheduled.

The ride home was filled with silence. Fear filled my body. The thoughts just would not let go of all the things that could happen. Had we worn out our welcome with asking God for prayers?

It seemed as if time passed fast, and we were back at the hospital again, only this time it was to have Bob's lungs examined by a lung specialist. Remember I told you before that the doctor didn't like or want Bob sedated because of his liver; however, there wasn't any other way to do this except to sedate him and have him fully under. The trip to the hospital was in silence. I knew Bob and I were thinking about the same things. How would we both survive this next venture into his illness and disease? We reached the hospital and moved in silence. We waited in the waiting room for them to call out

Bob's name. It wasn't a long wait before they made the call or came for Bob. I wanted to go back with him to hold his hand to be there for him when he could not be there for himself. But the doctors wouldn't allow it. I waited in the waiting room with the other two people. It seemed like it took a long time for someone to come back and talk to me. All the people waiting had gone now, and it was just me in the cold, silent room. Just as I finished (what seemed) my hundredth prayer, the door flew open. The nurse told me that they had just brought him back to the recovery area and that the doctors would be out to talk to me in a little while. I had not seen Bob yet when two doctors—a man and a woman in white coats—arrived at the door to the waiting room. They came in and took a seat next to me. They introduced themselves, but I don't remember their names. I was just waiting for them to tell me the outcome. It looked like the woman doctor had been crying. I thought that tears were still in the corners of her eyes. She was the one that spoke to me first. Her hands were in her lap folded when she started the conversation.

"Mrs. Stemmler," she said, "the surgery went well, but the findings are not good. Your husband has stage IV lung cancer."

I immediately began to scream. "No, no, no."

The man sitting next to her took my hands and said, "We are so very, very sorry to have to give you this news."

My tears just kept coming more and more. I could not catch my breath. The woman handed me a tissue and took over the conversation again.

"I know you have questions, but we need to get back to our other patients, so if we could get to the questions, please?"

I struggled to speak. "How long does he have to live?"

"This is March," the man sitting next to me said, "and if your husband is lucky, he could live to the end of May."

If lucky. My thoughts stuck on his words Lucky? Nothing had been lucky for Bob and me up to this point. It had all been built on hope, God, and prayer.

I asked them, "Did you tell him about the diagnosis?"

"No," they said. "He is not awake yet. He is in recovery; you will have to tell him."

Again, they said, "We need to get back to our other surgeries and our other patients." At that point, both of them got up.

They asked, "Are there any more questions, Mrs. Stemmler?"

There were a million questions or thoughts going through my head.

Then my voice cracked as I asked, "How will I tell him?"

"It will be okay," they said, with hope in their voices. "It will be okay. You will find a way to make him understand."

They both shook my hand, one after another, and then left the waiting room. I had had some pretty awful news about Bob in the past when dealing with his liver; however, I never knew or never thought this would be the outcome of this visit to the hospital today.

I stayed in the waiting room trying to gain my thoughts back and trying to find the right words to tell Bob what was going on and what the doctors had found. I took the time to pray and ask God for the strength to find the right words. I took the time to wipe the tears from my face. I took the time to thank God for all he had done for us in the past. Then, with the help of the walls as a leaning post, I got myself up out of my chair and walked out the door into the recovery room. I found Bob still asleep from the anesthetic. I just took his warm hand and stood beside him until he came back to me. His glassy blue eyes spoke with urgency.

"What's going on?" he said. "What did the doctors have to say? What did the doctors find? Can I go home?"

The one thing Bob never said was, "I'm hungry. Can I eat?" Those were always his words after he came out from under anesthesia.

I took one question at a time.

"It's not good, hon. The doctors found your lungs are full of cancer, not just cancer but stage four cancer." He took a moment.

"I'm not sure we can fight this battle by ourselves," he said, crying and squeezing my hand. This is not the kind of battle we have ever fought by ourselves. We have always had hope, faith, and God with us."

I just knew that this disease, called cancer, was bigger than anything else, and it would be a long road.

I took my husband home that day knowing there would have to be a new plan—a new plan to keep him alive with his liver failure and with cancer. We would have to decide what would be best for his liver and what help we could get for cancer. Bob just knew he could have treatment, so we set up an appointment with the Siteman cancer hospital. He wanted the appointment as soon as possible, so we called and made it for the next week.

As we entered the doctor's office, the doctor sat down with us to explain what choices Bob had as far as treatment.

She said that if he had chemo, it would affect the liver. If he did have chemo, it would be such a small amount that she didn't even think it would help. Bob found some hope in her words that day, so he set out to make a big decision whether to have chemo or not. I was against chemo because I knew what his liver had gone through before and what his liver was going through now, and I knew his liver could not keep up with the chemo. But I did not want to take the hope away from my husband that day. So I just listened. He kept asking me my opinion, so I kept telling him the truth. I never lied to him. For the first time, this made him angry.

We set out to make the final arrangements just like we knew what time—what day and what hour—Bob would leave this earth. He just had to be in control and ahead of this disease—this thing called cancer.

He wanted to take the last fishing trip, but I knew he couldn't put the boat in the water by himself. So I asked him if he would ask our son and grandson to go with him. He said that would be fine. Of course, Banjo never left his side unless he was at the hospital or at the doctor's office, so Bob set out for his last fishing trip destination to be the lake of the Ozarks. Bob loved his boat and everything fishing—his fishing poles and the joy it gave him to slow him down in life. We still did not have much money at that time, even though I was still working. Some days I took off without pay. I took $300 and gave it to him and hoped that would be enough. It saddens me that that's all we had to spare for him to have his final trip. I wish it could've been more, but it just wasn't there to be had, and someone in the family had to be practical. We had a long road before us, and we did not know what that road would entail. This was all new water for us to tread. Bob, Tim, and Blaine took the boat to the lake in the Ozarks. Bob constantly called me wanting me to change my mind about him having chemo. He wanted my blessings. He did not want to do this just with him making all the decisions. It was hard for me, but I told him to go ahead and do what he needed to do for him, and I would stand by his side no matter what happened. Bob came back, and we set up an appointment with Siteman Cancer Center. On Bob's first appointment, the drug dose they put into his system was so small it looked like a bubble in an eyedropper, but that was enough for Bob because he knew, he just knew, it was enough to cure him. He had fought many battles of life and some with scars; he was proud of the scars, but this was one fight we both knew was just beneath hope. Bob managed to get through the first round of chemo. How he did this I'll never know. The treatments seemed to be a little bit better—a little bit better from sickness, better with hope, and a little bit better knowing he had one round completed, and it might be all he needed. That wasn't the case. After the second round of chemo, Bob's liver started failing. He got weaker and weaker. His ammonia levels were on the rise, and the chemo made him so sick he started throwing up. He was back to throwing up blood again. Only this time the cause was chemo.

Bob had less and less oxygen in his body because his lungs were being taken over by cancer. His breathing became harder and harder. He would put nasal strips across his nose hoping this would help him breathe. I would ask him if it helped; he would say it did.

We talked about the final arrangements and about where he wanted to be taken if he passed. He wanted to be cremated, and if he passed in St. Louis, he wanted to be taken to a St. Louis crematory. If he passed in Washington, he wanted to be taken to the crematory in Washington. He also wanted his ashes spread over the Current River. We talked about the cost of the cremation. It was $1,500. We had managed to save this money and put it aside. Bob wanted to die at home, and if that was a part of his last wishes, I would stand by them. However, when the day came, Bob became really weak, and it was evident that we were both scared.

He called my name from the bedroom, He said, "Will you help me get to the bathroom?"

I had carried Bob several times before because his weight had gone down so fast, and he was so weak, but now it seemed that I was just carrying a shell of a man—a shell that couldn't be much more than sixty-five to ninety pounds.

I put him back in bed, and he looked up at me and said, "You're really scared, aren't you?"

I said, "I just don't stop praying; I know God is with us, but I just think we can do more for you if you go to the hospital."

He said, "Call the doctor and tell him what's going on."

I picked up the phone and dialed his number; it was always on speed dial. I explained the situation and what was going on. "He is so much weaker; he can't take any air in, and we are both very scared!"

The doctor said, "Get him to the hospital, Brenda."

I told Bob we needed to go to the hospital, and I needed to call the ambulance.

He said, "Okay, but don't call the police. I won't fight you this time."

The ambulance attendants came and put Bob on the gurney. They wheeled Bob out of the house and into the ambulance. I told them I would follow them. I had Bob's paperwork and his last will and testament and his living will in my hands. They said, "No, you will not follow us; you will ride with us."

I believe after taking Bob's vitals they really knew ... They did not want Bob to die without me. The attendant had taken Bob's vitals when he entered the bedroom and told me that his oxygen levels were very low; the other man took me aside and told me that they did not know how he was still breathing.

They left the window between the front and back open as they transported, so I could talk to Bob. Where are we transporting him? Barnes Jewish Hospital. The driver tried to keep my mind off what was going on in the back. We got to the hospital, and they put Bob in a waiting room. It seemed like it took hours and hours for them to get him any help. I believe they knew he wasn't going anywhere, and he definitely wasn't going home. I stayed with him throughout the night.

The social worker came in and said, "You need to go home and get some rest."

I assured her that I was okay. I just told her I needed coffee; she pointed to the coffee room and told me to go in there anytime I wanted. She also gave me instructions to the chapel. I knew the chapel would be the first stop.

I asked the nurse if I could I leave him for a while.

She said, "He is stable, as stable as we can get him. You need to take care of yourself."

I proceeded to the chapel. There, I asked God for Bob to bear no more pain and for him to just let go and let God have him. He had been through so much, and, as I said before, he was just a shell of a body—a shell of a man. Bob never wanted to be down this close to death where he couldn't be fishing with Banjo. I cried and cried. But I wiped my eyes and left the chapel knowing it was all up to God, and I would have to be stronger now.

I went home for three hours. It took an hour to get there and an hour to get back, so I stayed at home an hour and took a shower. I never rested but gathered Bob's clothes just like I would be bringing him home. Just like I always did. I got ready for the doctors to make him better so I could take him home.

Bob and I were alone in the hospital room, and I looked at his hand, and he didn't have his wedding ring on. I asked him where his wedding ring was, and he said he didn't know.

I knew I'd seen his wedding ring on his finger. He never took it off before we went to the hospital, but it wasn't there now. I went to the nurse's desk and told them that his wedding ring wasn't on his finger, and it was missing. They said they would ask the ambulance attendants if they had seen it, and they would keep a lookout for it. I felt like I was accusing someone of stealing Bob's ring, but then after I got home, I pulled back the bedsheets to see what I needed to clean up, and there in the middle—right in the center—of the bed was Bob's wedding ring, and the first thing that I could think of was *till death do us part*. I believe Bob had left his wedding ring there because he knew he was never coming home. He had given up. I believe he wanted me to have it as a keepsake. I believe, as we both knew, everything came full circle. I cried and screamed and beat the bed with both fists, knowing that he knew he was never coming home again. He would never see Banjo again. He would never fish again. He would never see his children or his grandchildren again, and we would never dance again. I wiped my eyes on the bedsheets and pulled myself up to take a shower. I needed to get back to him.

I got back to his room and put the clothes I brought for him in the drawer beside his bed, just like I always did. Bob was sitting up eating orange sherbet ice cream; it was his favorite. He was trying to eat it with a plastic spoon. I asked him if he needed help, and he didn't say anything. I just took the spoon from his hand and put a metal spoon in his hand. He didn't want me to help him. He threw the spoon and took the plastic spoon back. His eyes had changed colors. You could hardly see the white. His face was drawn, and his hands shook as he desperately tried to spoon the ice cream out of the Styrofoam cup. The nurse had passed me in the hall and told me Bob was doing fine, and she had just been in to see him. This did not look like my husband in this hospital bed, and fine was not what I was seeing. The aide was by his bedside.

He asked the aide if she would straighten his pillow up.

She said, "Sure, Mr. Stemmler."

She looked at me and asked, "Would you help me pull him up."

I did not have one bit of strength left. I tried to help her, but I just couldn't do it. She started to lower his bed, and then it happened. Green fluids came out of his nose, his mouth, his ears, and his eyes. I yelled and screamed and ran to the hallway to get help. The nurses and doctors came running. I started to run back into Bob's room, but the nurse grabbed my arm and positioned me against the hall wall. Code blue was what I heard all over again. It echoed through the hallways—code blue, code blue—and buzzers kept going off. I stood there where the nurse left me, helpless. The social worker came running. She screamed, "I will get the chaplain."

I knew then something was not right. I kept screaming and screaming.

Bob had made it a point to write in his living will that he did not want to be revived. He had put in his living will that he did not want his family to do a final viewing. (He did not want his family to go through any more pain). He had also put in his living will that if he could not do the things he loved to do, like fishing and dancing with me, then let him go.

I knew when I heard the buzzers going off and the cart coming down the hallway that they were going to revive him. He did not want this, and I kept screaming at them to listen. I kept waving the paper in front of everyone who passed. He did not want this! The nurse told me, "We don't have his living will." I kept trying to show them I had it. The chaplain came and stood beside me. He asked, "Would you like to pray with me?"

But before the chaplain had arrived, there was a man standing next to me the whole time. He was leaning against the wall with me. A man wearing a tan or beige suit. It was the same man standing with me in the trauma center that night when I was fighting for my husband's life. The same man that was telling me I was the only one to fight because my husband was not strong enough to help himself. The soft-spoken man supporting me and giving me the will and strength to help Bob.

With the same soft voice now, he was assuring me it would be okay. He assured me that God was with Bob. He assured me that I did all the right things. He assured me that Bob was in the right place. He told me I would keep making the right decisions. His last words to me were, "You are a strong woman, and your husband loves you. Your spirit is strong and your faith even stronger. You will be okay."

Bob had made the comment that he did not want his family there. We had talked about this so many times. I had been there several years back, with my own son struggling to hold onto life, and I knew from a mother's eyes that I would want to see my son for the last time.

I chose a different path than what Bob wanted, but after praying about my choice, I knew what I had to do. I chose to call his family.

I called Bob's sister Kathy. She came with her sister, Dottie, and I'm sure they called others. As they walked down the hall, my tears flooded the hallway.

They did not look at me, but I said, "He is gone."

Dottie said as she passed, "I know our brother was hard to love."

She and Kathy entered Bob's room. It was not long, and both of them reentered the hallway. I still think about Dottie's words. I knew Bob was never hard to love. That was the easy part of our marriage.

After standing there for a while with the chaplain, I started talking to the man who stood beside me.

The chaplain asked, "Who are you talking to?"

I said, "I'm talking to the man standing next to me."

He said, "There is no one there, Mrs. Stemmler." I turned away to look beside me where the man had been standing against the wall. He was not there.

I knew he had just been there, but the chaplain said, "I never saw anyone."

The same man that was in the trauma center coaching me to fight for my husband's life was standing next to me that day as my husband took his last breaths.

Bob was a fighter; he fought for anything he believed in

and for things he didn't believe in, but he loved life to the fullest. He actually relabeled life in a sense; his definition was way broader than anyone I had ever met. We were young at heart, young at loving, and young with God's will.

You know there is a saying that most people say after someone passes, especially if you've lost a husband or a child, or anyone for that matter. "I'm sorry," they say, and they give their sympathy, and they hold your hand, and they say they can feel your pain. They know this because they have felt pain, but to me, that's not true. No one can label or measure; nor can they tell what someone else is going through. No one can tell you how long it takes to grieve. It is your road to go down for however long it takes you to get there. It is a road all your own. It is a journey with you and God.

The hospital staff put Bob in a private viewing room that day after they hooked him up to all the machines. They wanted the family to have a private place to be when they said their final words to Bob. A private place to view his last breaths. A private place to listen to his heartbeat after they turned off the machines. Bob had a strong heart. His heart was the best part of him because he loved with his whole heart. He lived with a strong heart, and he prayed with a strong heart. I believe that was why it took over an hour for him to pass and his heart to stop beating. I stood there holding his warm hand. His face showed no pain. There were no wrinkles on his hand or face—no evidence of his struggles hours and days before. The only sign of life was his heart beating. I know I had made the decision to call Bob's family, but a warm feeling and their faces told me that it was the right call. My thoughts went blank as the last buzzer went off signaling the nurses and doctors to reenter the room. My son walked up beside me and took my hand from Bob's hand. He ushered me out the door and to a chair. His words came with a tearful voice and comfort. "Mom," he said, "Dad is gone."

Something inside me snapped. I started throwing up, and my grandson ran for a waste can. It felt like an explosion going off inside me. My son held my hand until the doctor came to announce Bob's time of death and to say that there would be papers to sign. I looked around for Bob's family, and Tim told me they were in the waiting room. What were they waiting for? Bob had passed, and that was his final trip to the hospital. Why were they waiting?

Through all Bob's sickness and through all of our love and through our marriage, Bob always had hope. Every time he would get sick he knew he could lean on hope and faith in God. However, when Bob was told he had stage IV cancer, I know if Bob could tell you, he'd say that hope had turned its back on the two of us. He always knew when I told him he had stage four cancer that his will to live was *just beneath hope*.

Watching Bob die that day was the worst thing that I have ever experienced. His illness and death took a part of me. I was so mad at the disease that I could not wait for exhaustion to leave me. I had to get rid of all the evidence of the disease that took my husband's life. I took down the bed. I took down the pictures. I boxed up all the clothes. I call my sons to come and get everything. I knew in doing this I was getting rid of the disease. I could smell the disease in every room. The only room I did not touch at that time was the garage. The garage was Bob's hiding place from the world. In this place, Bob sorted through his tools and made each son and his only grandson a toolbox. He put together two bikes—one for our granddaughter and one for our grandson. He made Banjo a rope to chew on and tied it from the garage rafters. Banjo would jump and try to get the knot at the end of the rope. He also sorted out his fishing poles and tackle for the boys to share. The last day he entered the garage was to hang his yellow shirt on the end of his workbench. This was the only piece of clothing that I had left that just smelled like Bob. It was the smell I knew when I would lie beside him each night. It took me a long time to clean out the garage and take Bob's yellow shirt off the end of the workbench. Some days I would go into the garage just to sniff the shirt. I did not want to lose the clean smell of him or to lose that memory. I just knew Bob would be looking down from heaven and saying, "Get a grip, honey."

During the next few days of cleaning the house, struggling

to *get a grip,* I was standing at the kitchen sink looking out the window, and an old fishing bobber was hanging from a limb. The warm tears rolled down my cheek. I just knew this was a sign from Bob and God. Bob was trying to tell me he was happy and fishing in heaven. God had kept his promise that all would be okay.

I know that people say you should wait at least two years before you get rid of stuff, but I just couldn't wait. I could not wait another day for cancer to live in our home.

Most people would say it was crazy, and they would probably be right by saying that; however, I didn't feel a bit crazy. I knew what it took for me to live healthier, and it wasn't going to be looking at the things that the disease took from me. Cancer has a strength all its own; no one has figured out its power. No one has figured out how to get rid of the control it has over people. No one has figured out what it would take to cure it, so, in my own mind, I was getting rid of the disease of cancer. In my own mind, I was holding onto my own hope—the hope that with time I could move on. I still smell cancer on the few things I kept of Bob's.

The fishing bobber was not the only sign from God. There had been a note hanging on the icebox. A reminder for the appointment Bob made for me to take my cat to the vet. The appointment was scheduled for June 6—three days after Bob's passing. I just knew I had to keep going to get everything done before I needed to go back to work. I gathered up the cat, and we headed to the appointment. When I got there, much to my surprise, the cat had already had surgery. They had not taken care of it at this office. Was I losing my mind? Bob always wanted to take care of things while I was at work, but I knew in all the crazy, exhausted moments and hospital visits, this was one thing he had not shared with me that he had taken care of.

Bob and I had made all the plans for his arrangements. We talked about his last wishes. Even though he cared for his family, his last wishes to me were not to have them involved. However, Bob's sisters and his mother took Bob's remains—ashes—from the crematory. Therefore, I could not carry out Bob's last wishes. I do not have a place to visit him. I don't know for sure where they scattered the ashes or if they buried him. I allowed them to come to the hospital for their last viewing of their son and brother. I did not have the heart to refuse his mother the last chance to say goodbye to her son. Death has its own power over people.

Bob died five years ago, on June 3, 2013. I have not had any contact with his family since. I call, but I never leave a message. They still have Bob's voice on the answering machine. Bob's mother has lost her two sons, daughter, ex-husband, Bob's father, and her daughter-in-law. Three of those deaths were from cancer.

I hope in telling our story that someone will take something from it. My hope in writing was that it will help someone down the road take care of themselves when they are trying to take care of someone they love. I knew that I had to ask for help and that was the hardest thing for me to do. But I also believed that if I did not ask for help, we would not have what quality of life we had left together.

I could not quit working through all Bob's sickness. I was the only provider. I knew I had to take care of myself and him. I set out to do it all by myself the day the doctors told me Bob had stage four lung cancer. I soon learned I needed help and a plan. I put hospice in place, and I called the American Cancer Society. They helped with transporting Bob back and forth to his cancer treatments when I could not be there. I had a visiting nurse when needed. She would help sort out Bob's medication. I just did not want to get anything wrong. I knew this would be some load off my mind. I had meals on wheels delivered to the home. I made meals that Bob could handle by himself. I filled out paperwork for the Family Medical Leave Act if needed. This kept me from losing my job. We had a care team for each part of the facility where I worked, and I knew if I needed someone to talk to, they were there to help. I worked as a teacher for DEPARTMENT OF CORRECTIONS. Bob and I always made it through the rough parts of his sickness. My love for Bob was built on respect, honor, and keeping his dignity through all else. My hope and prayers are that they will find a cure for cancer, and no one ever has to live a life just beneath hope.

No one can love the depth you love.

No one can feel your life of pain.

No one can walk your path of grief.

No one can take your *hope* away.

It is our journey, but we are not alone.

Engagement picture

Bob's family: father, brother and wife.

About the Author

The Author is a mother, grandmother, a retired Special Needs Teacher and a writer. She published her first book in 2003 "Ocean's Anger". Her poetry was published in Best Poets of 2016, volume 5."

My writing and poetry is a way to give something back to other writers and poets. It is my own message to the world and my legacy.